SUPER CUTE FAIRIES & MERMAIDS

Fantasy Coloring Book

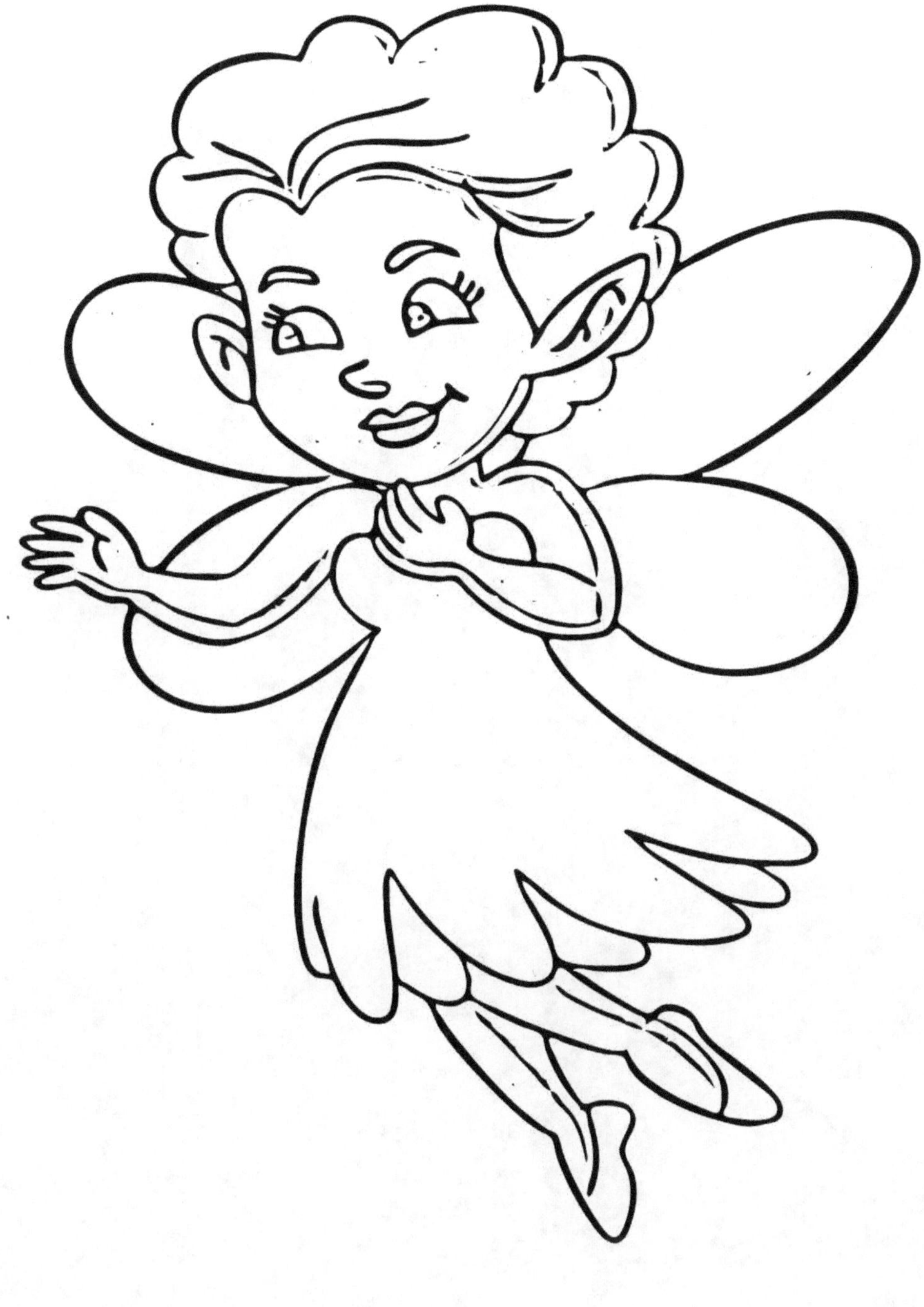

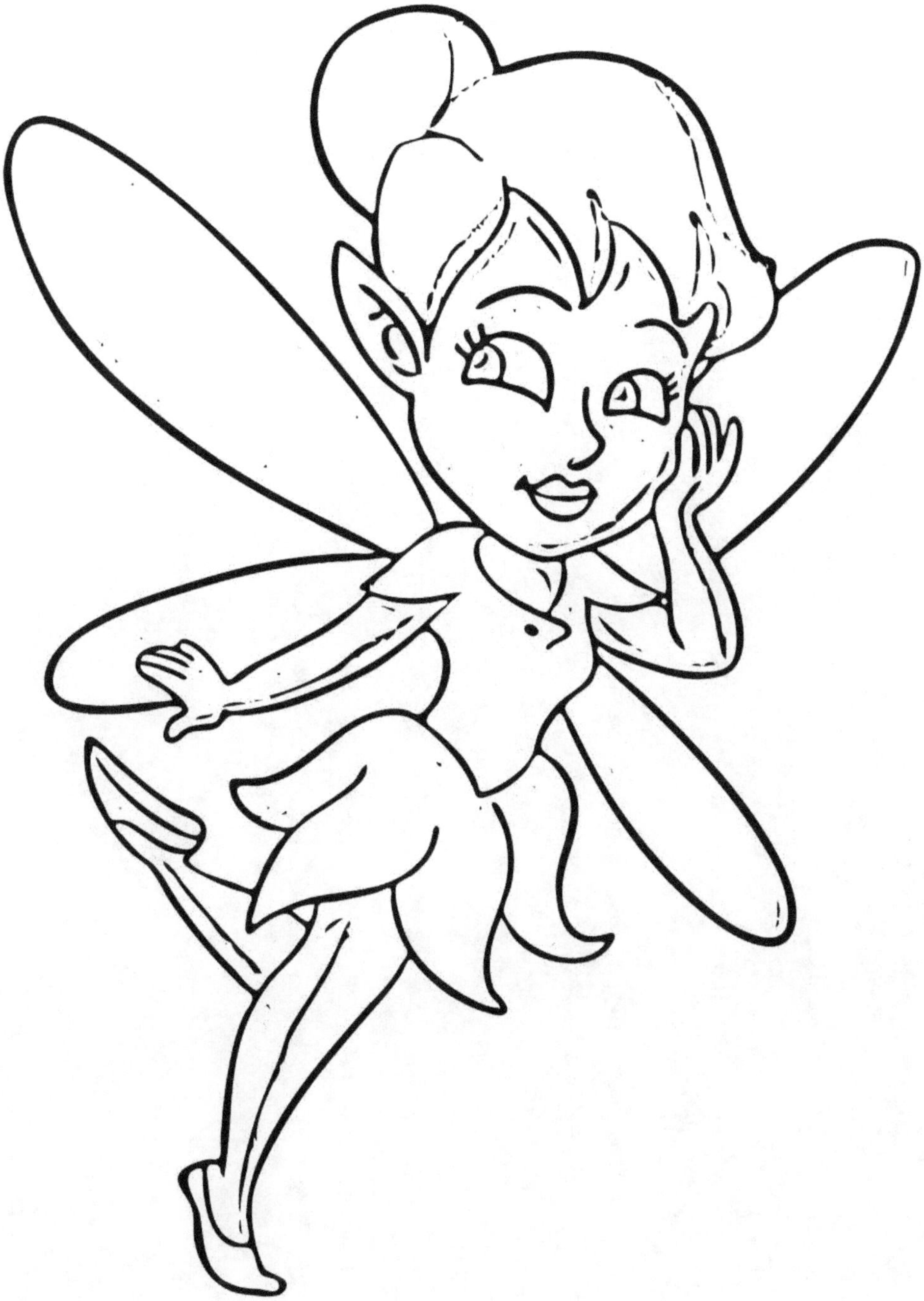

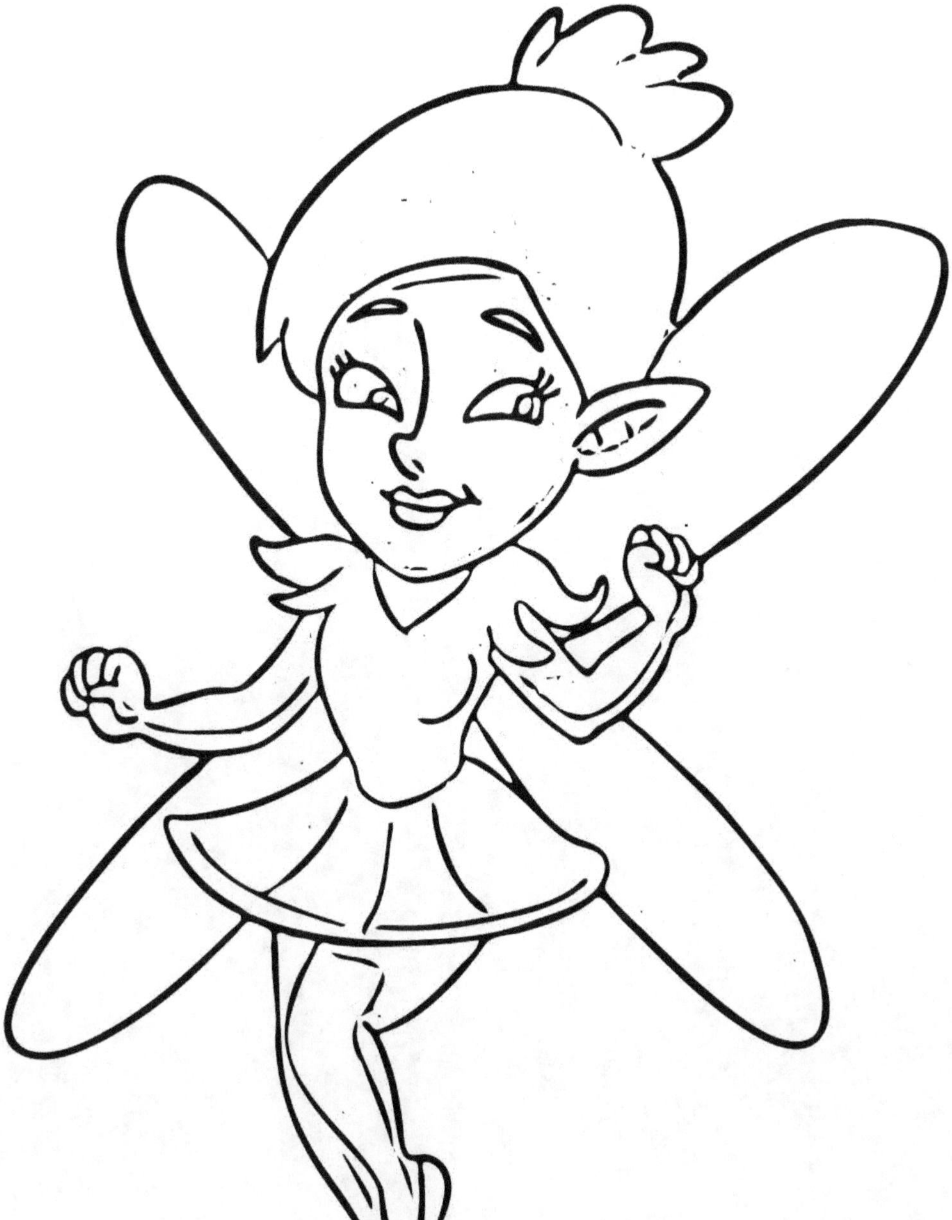

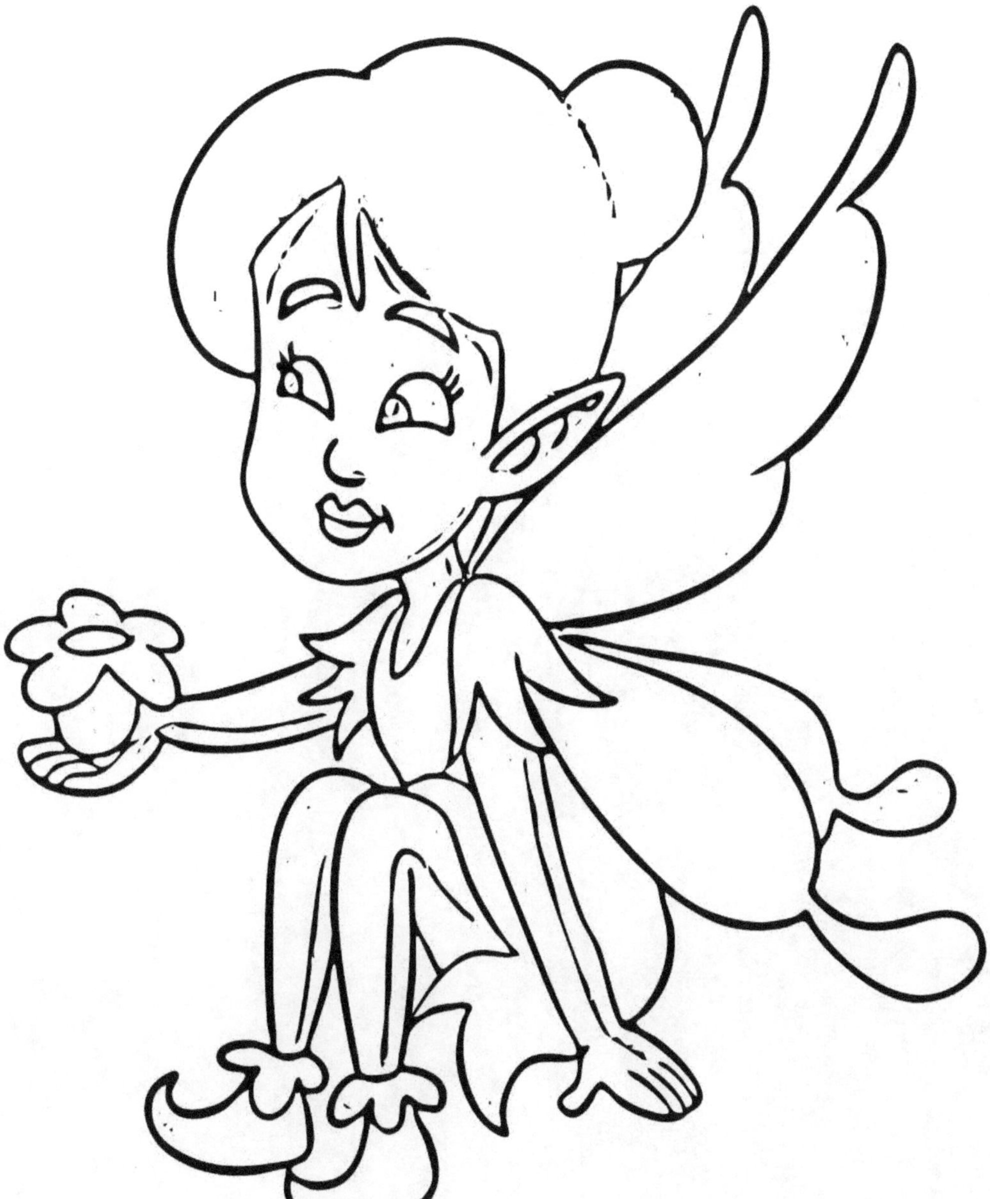

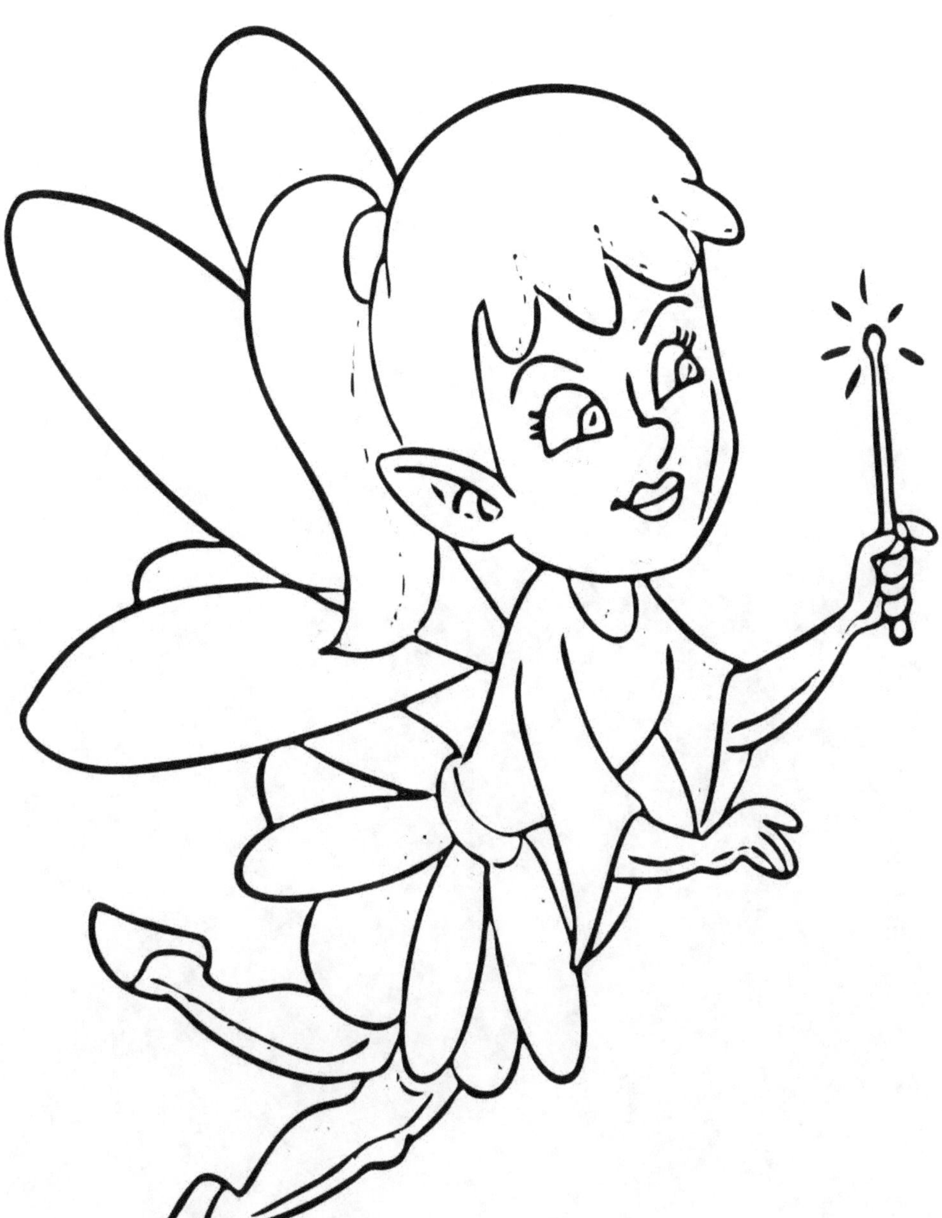

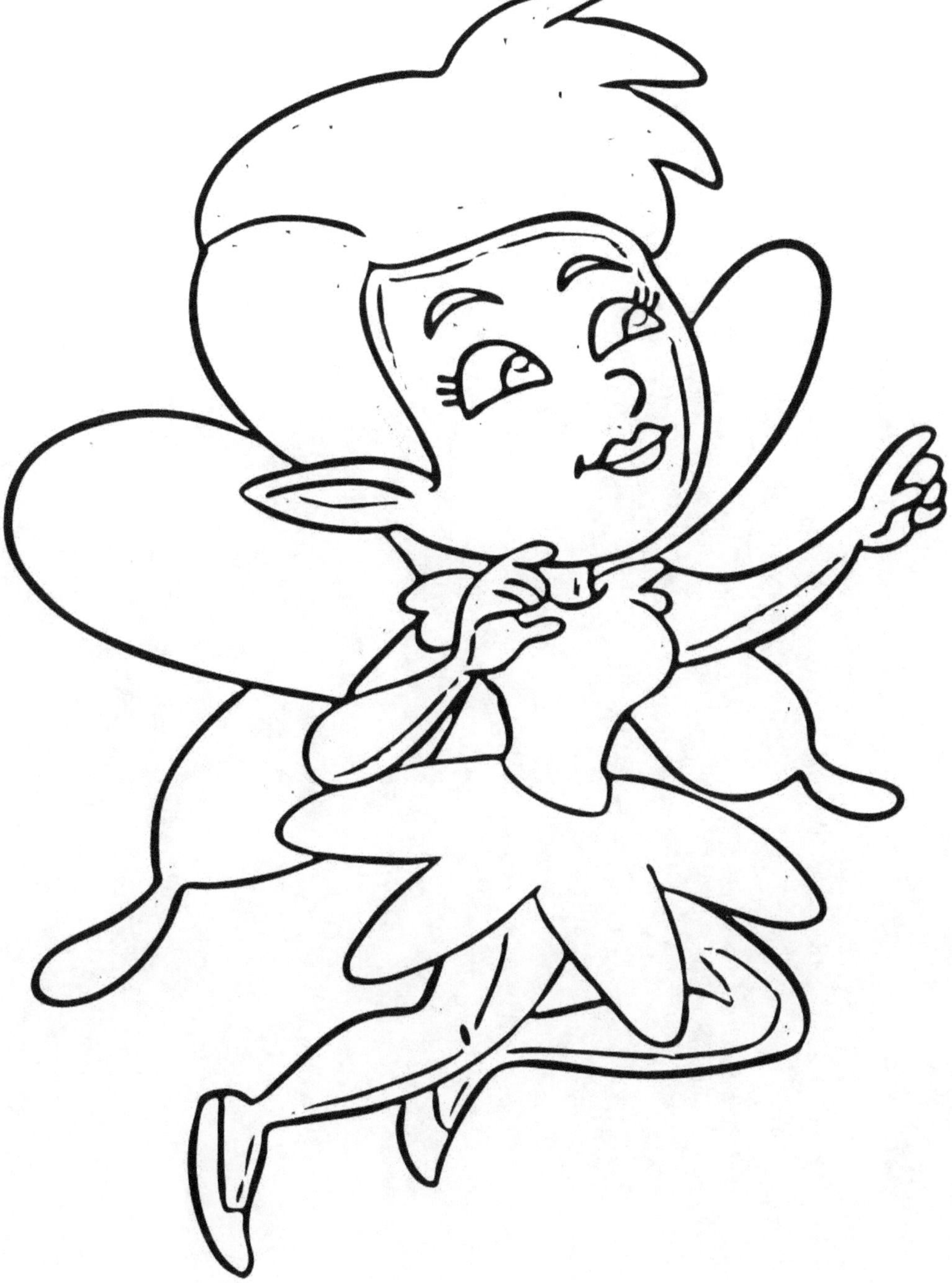

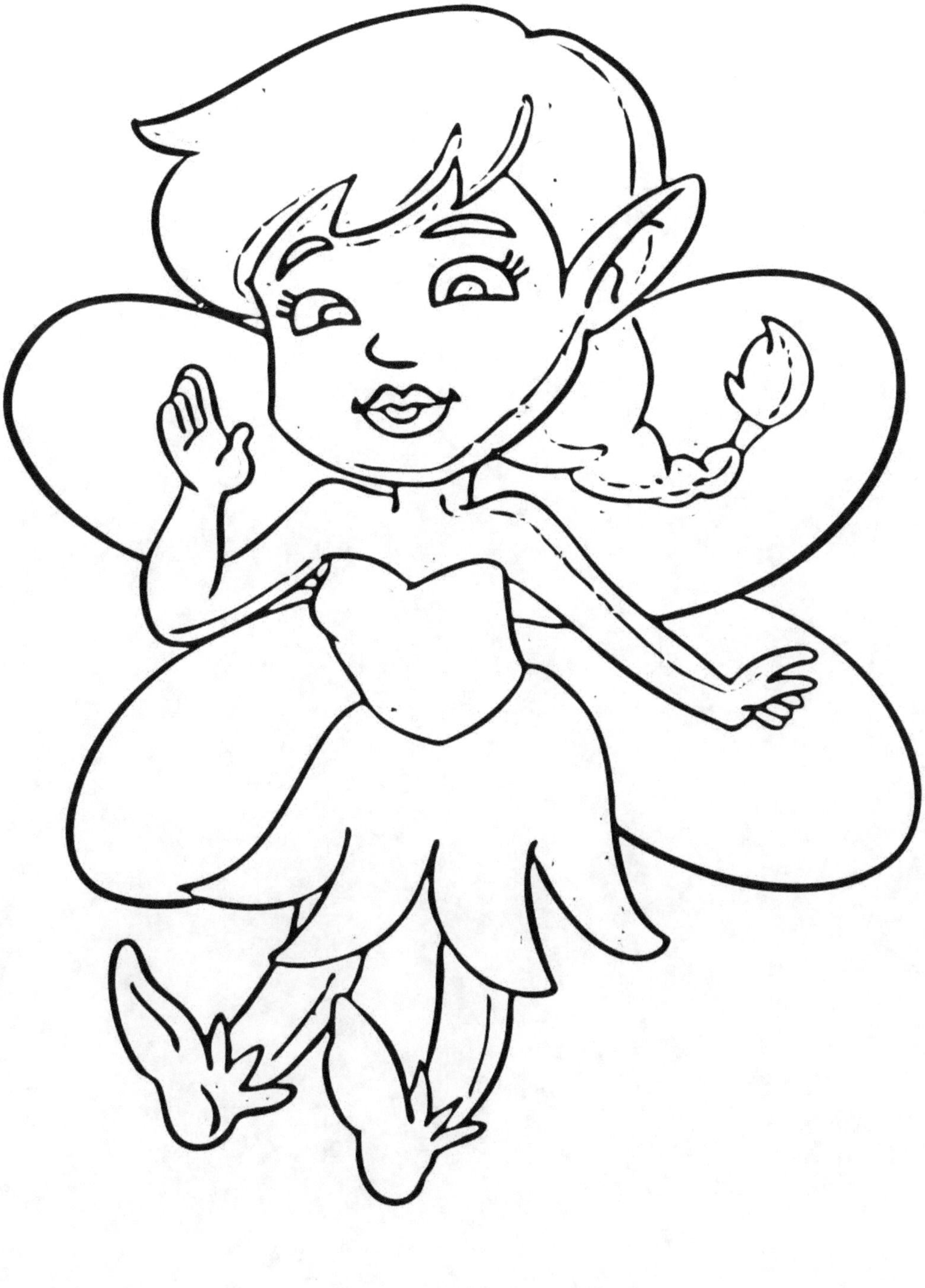

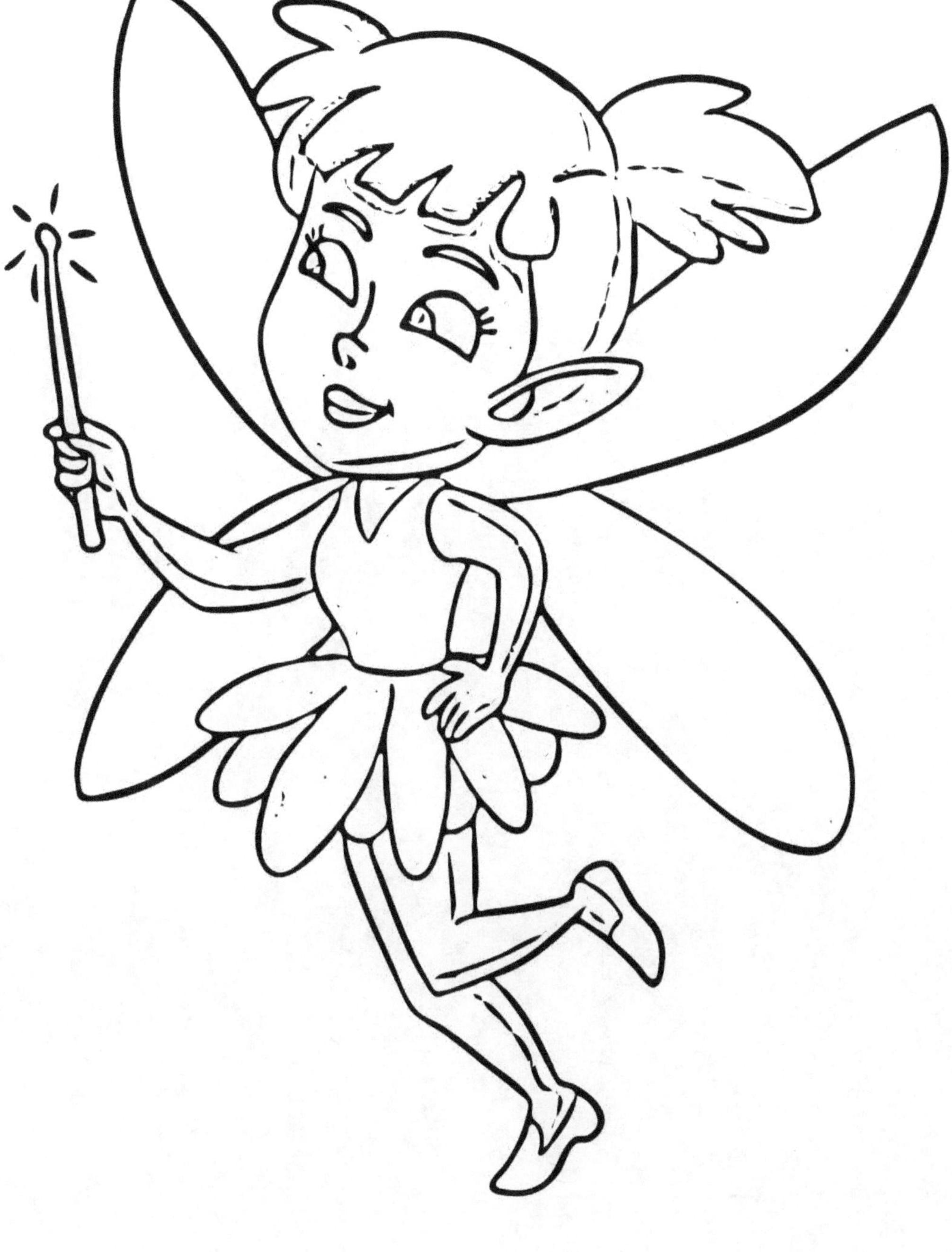

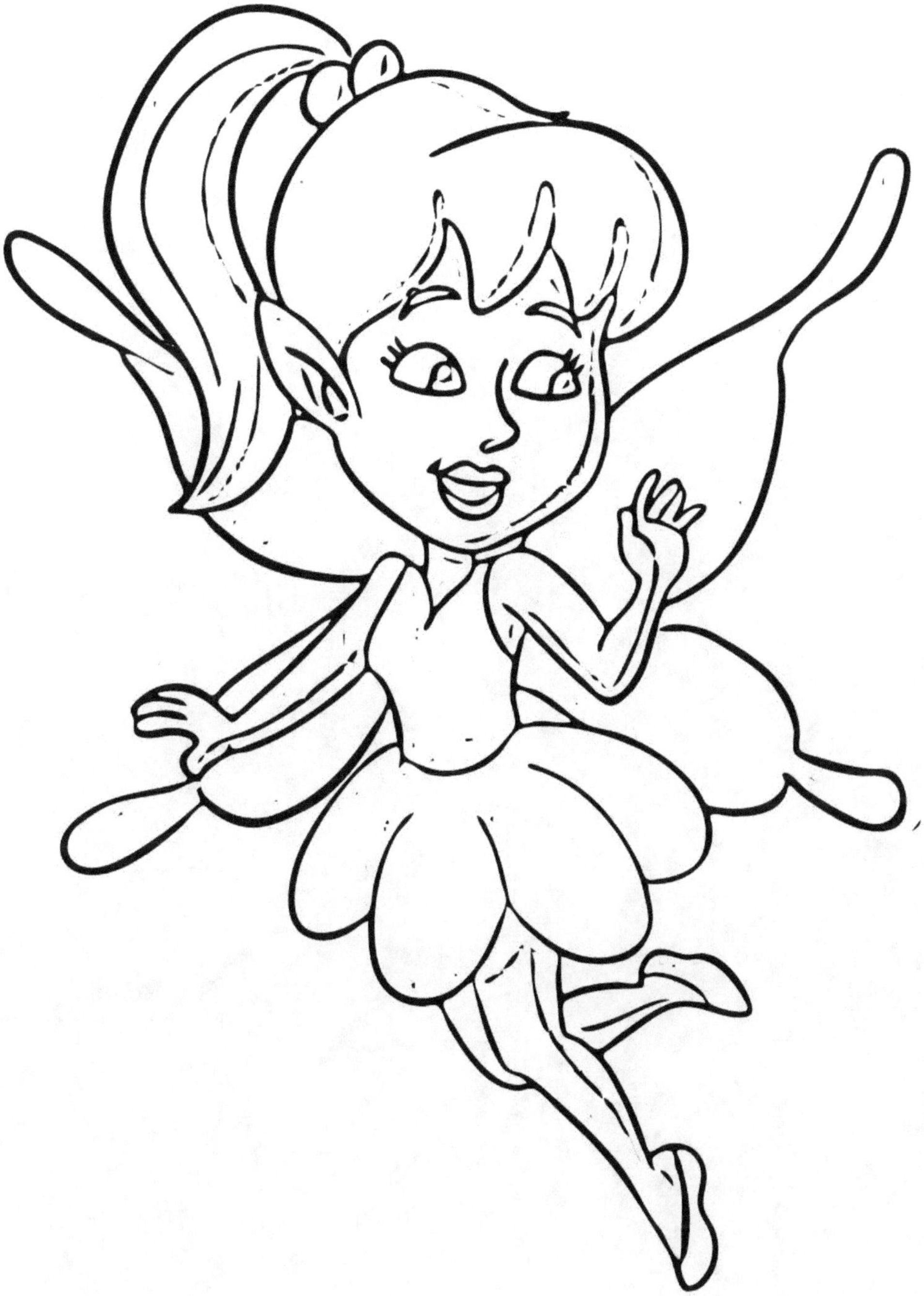

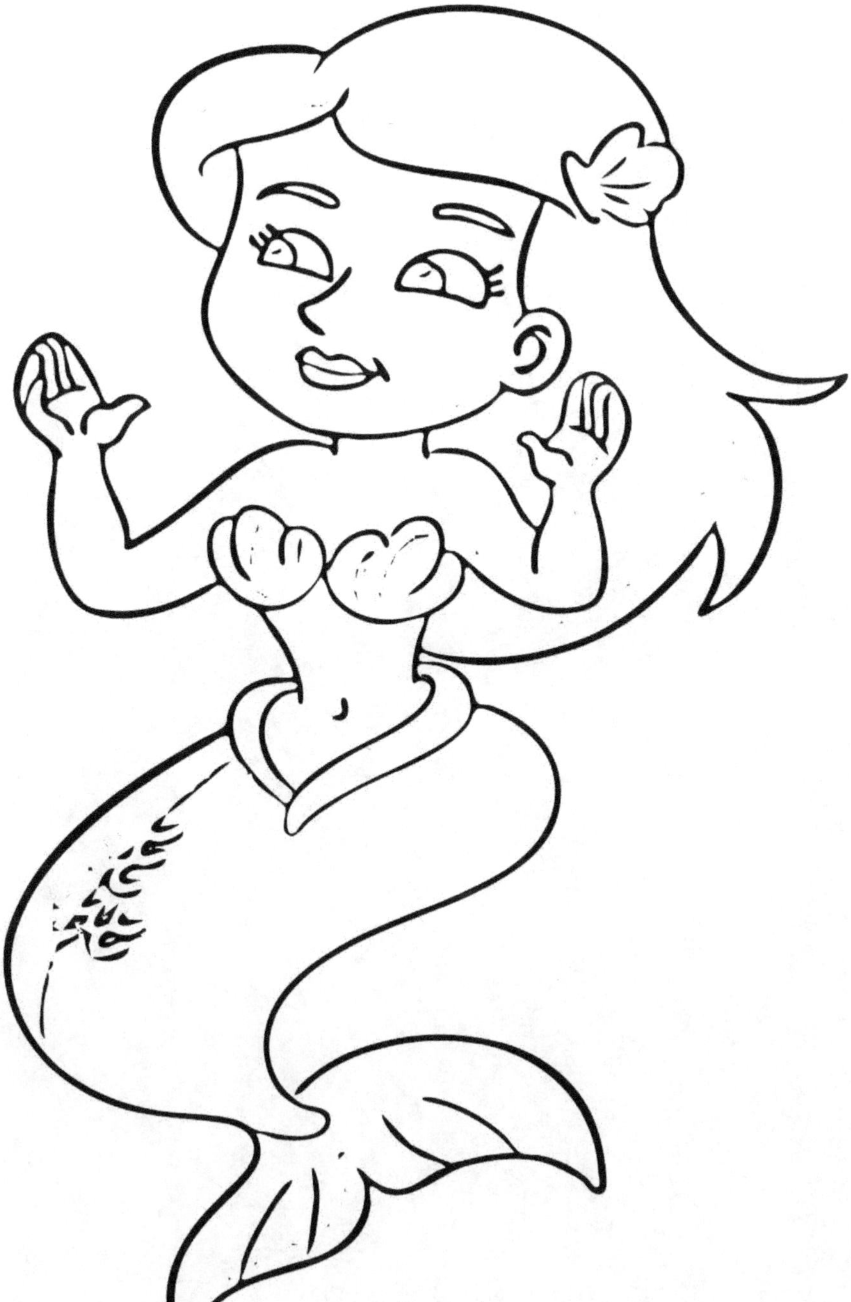

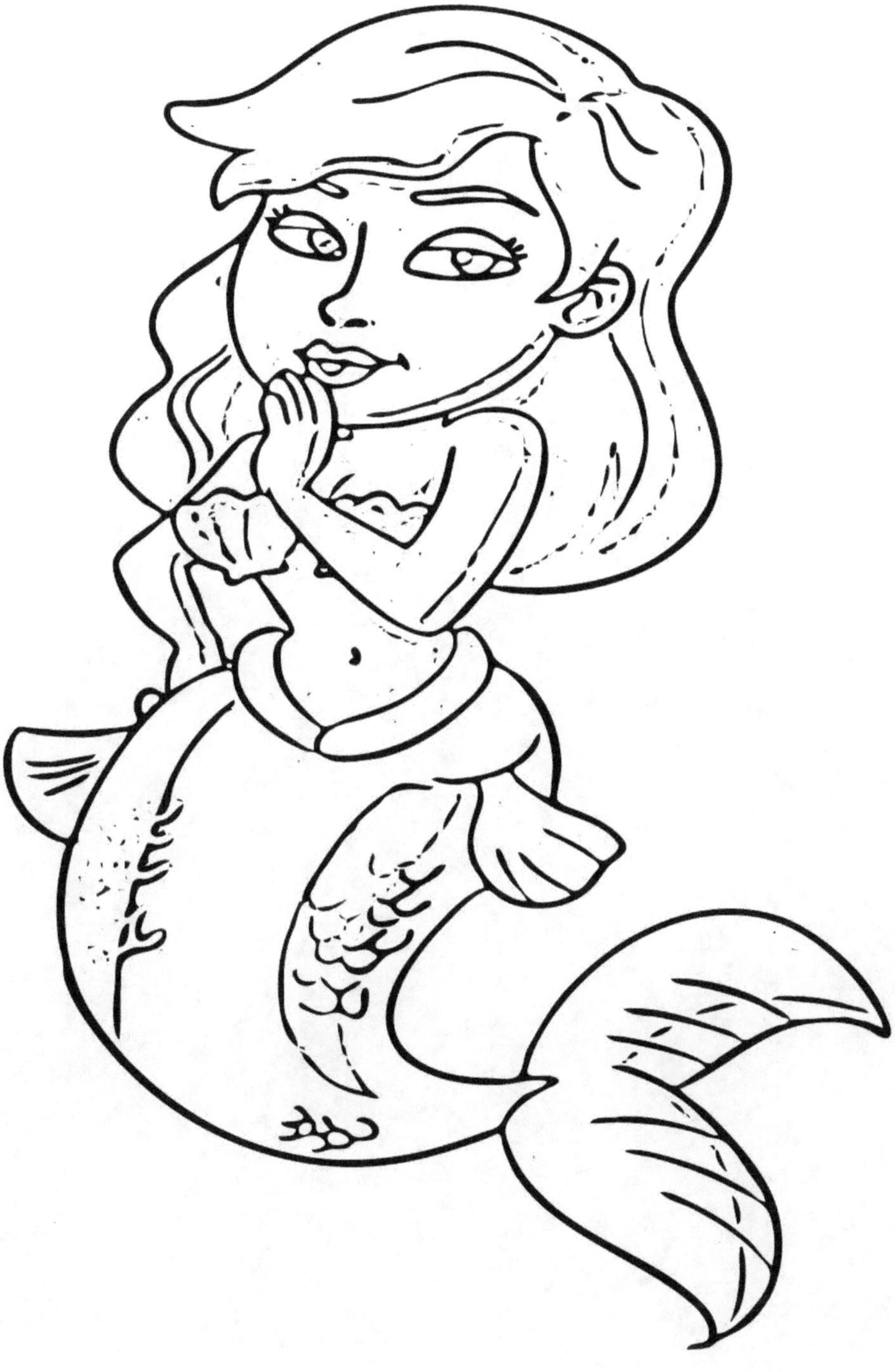

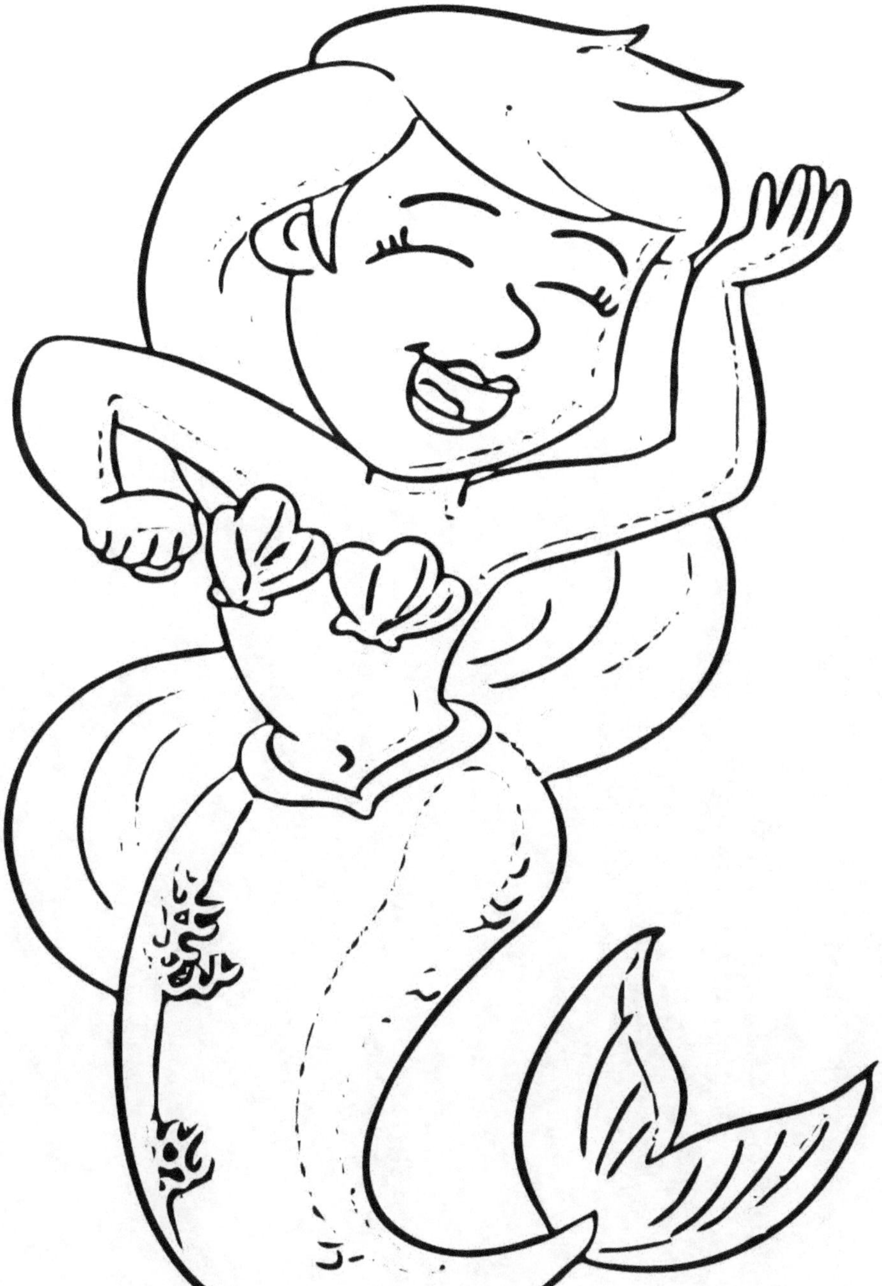

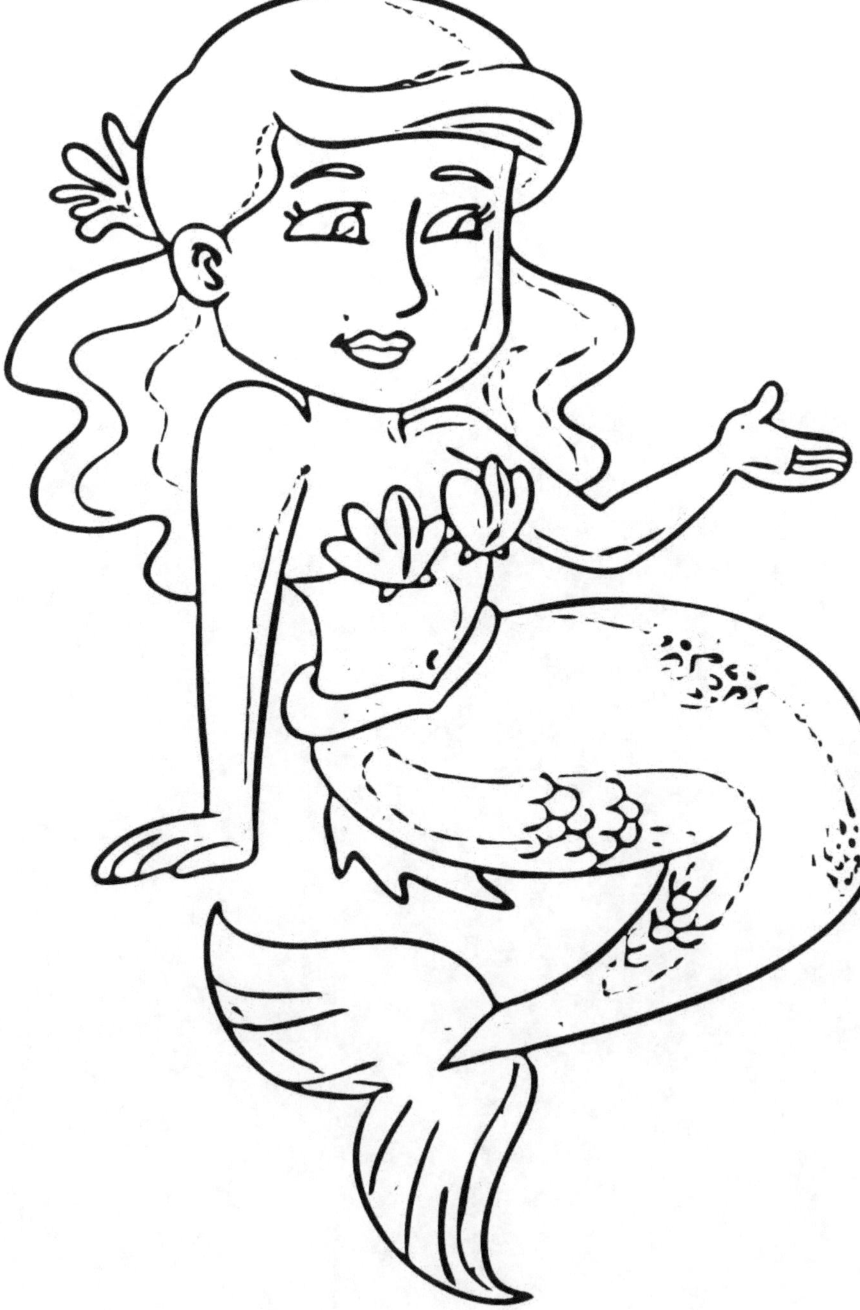

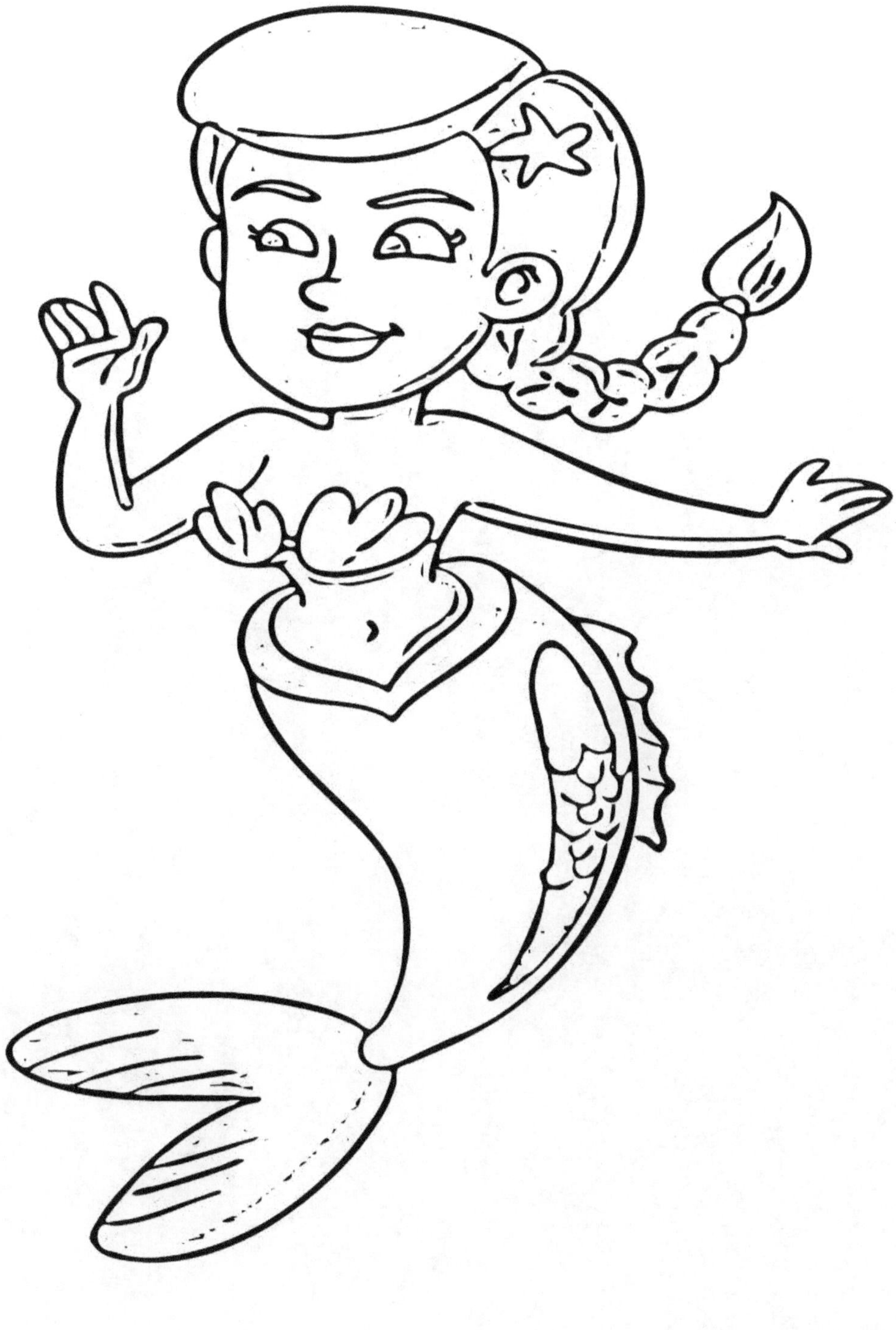

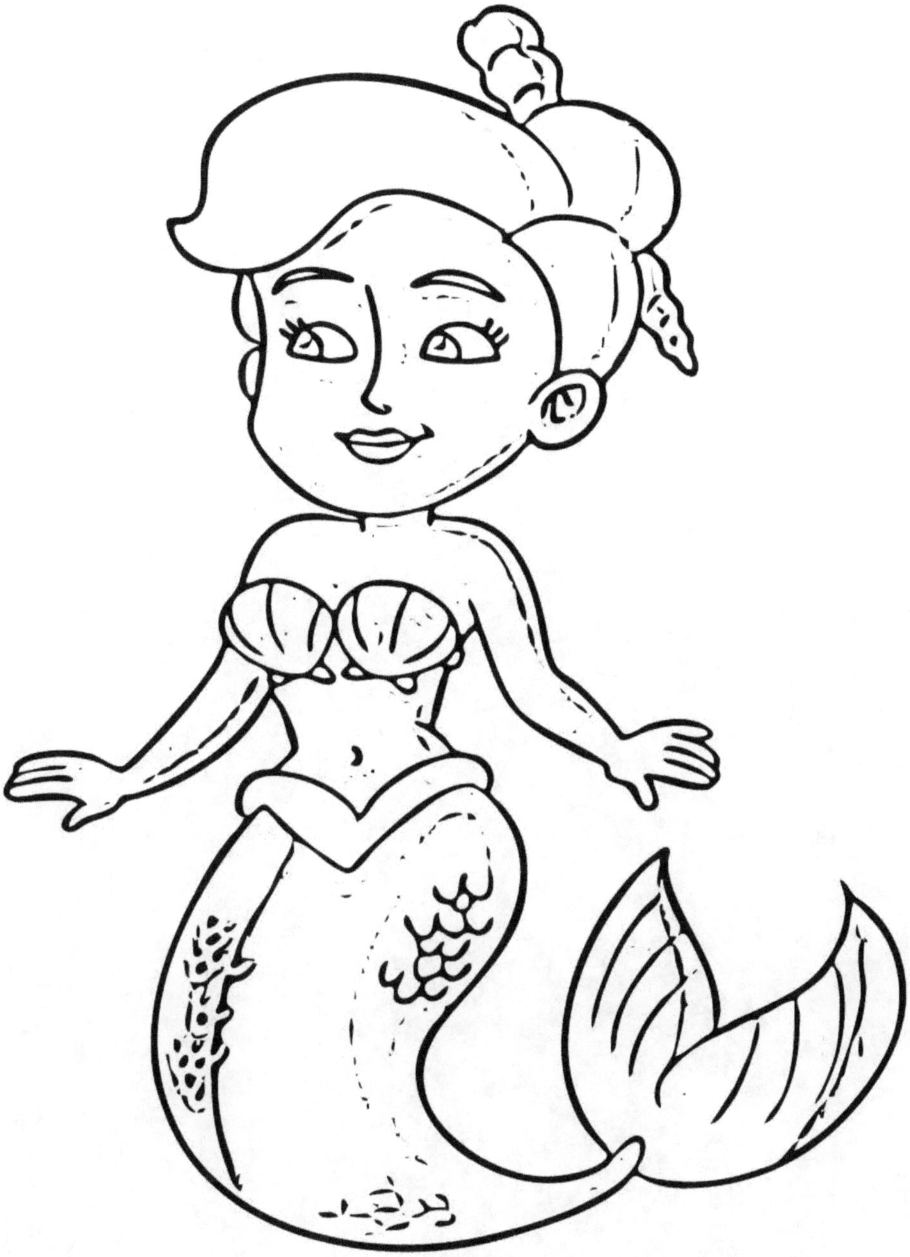

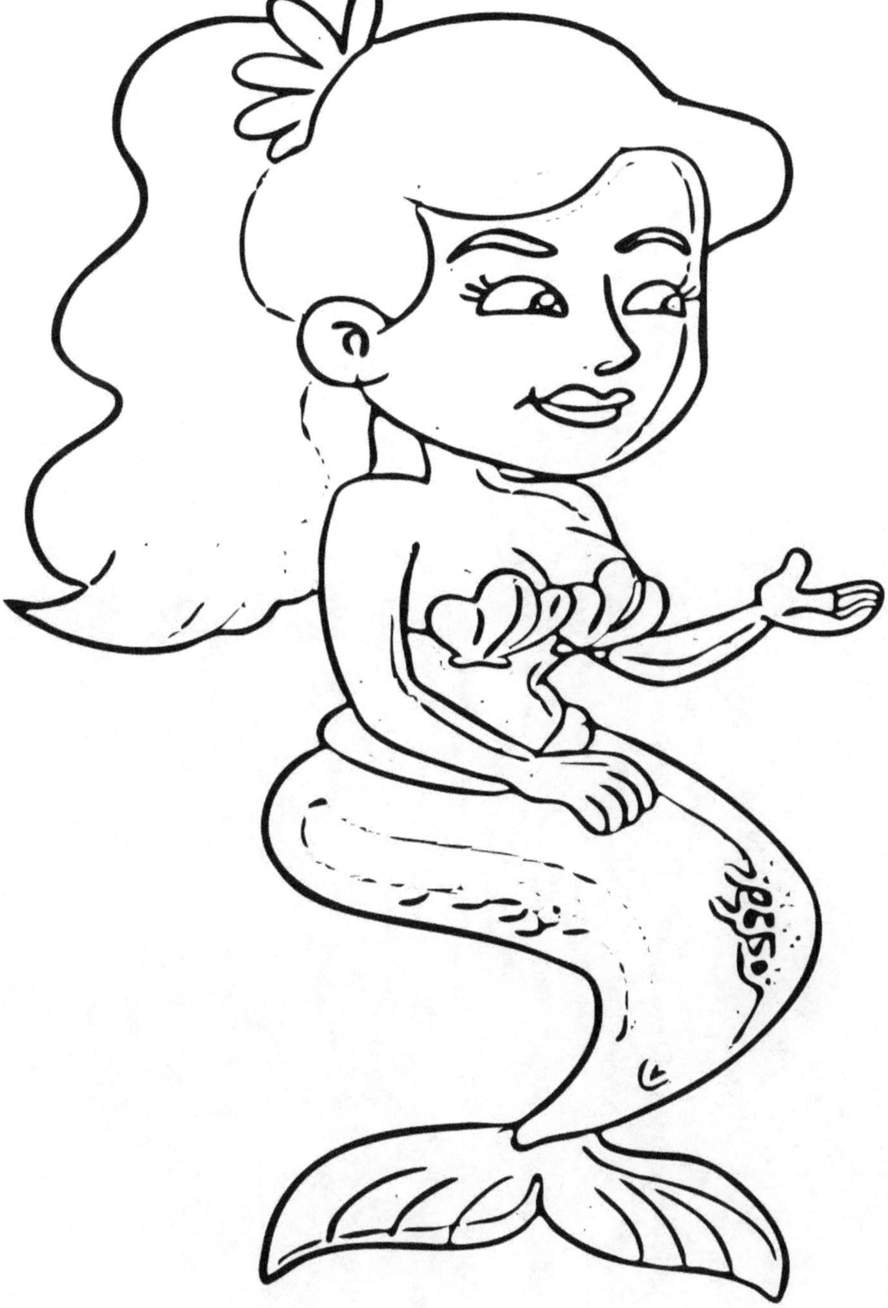

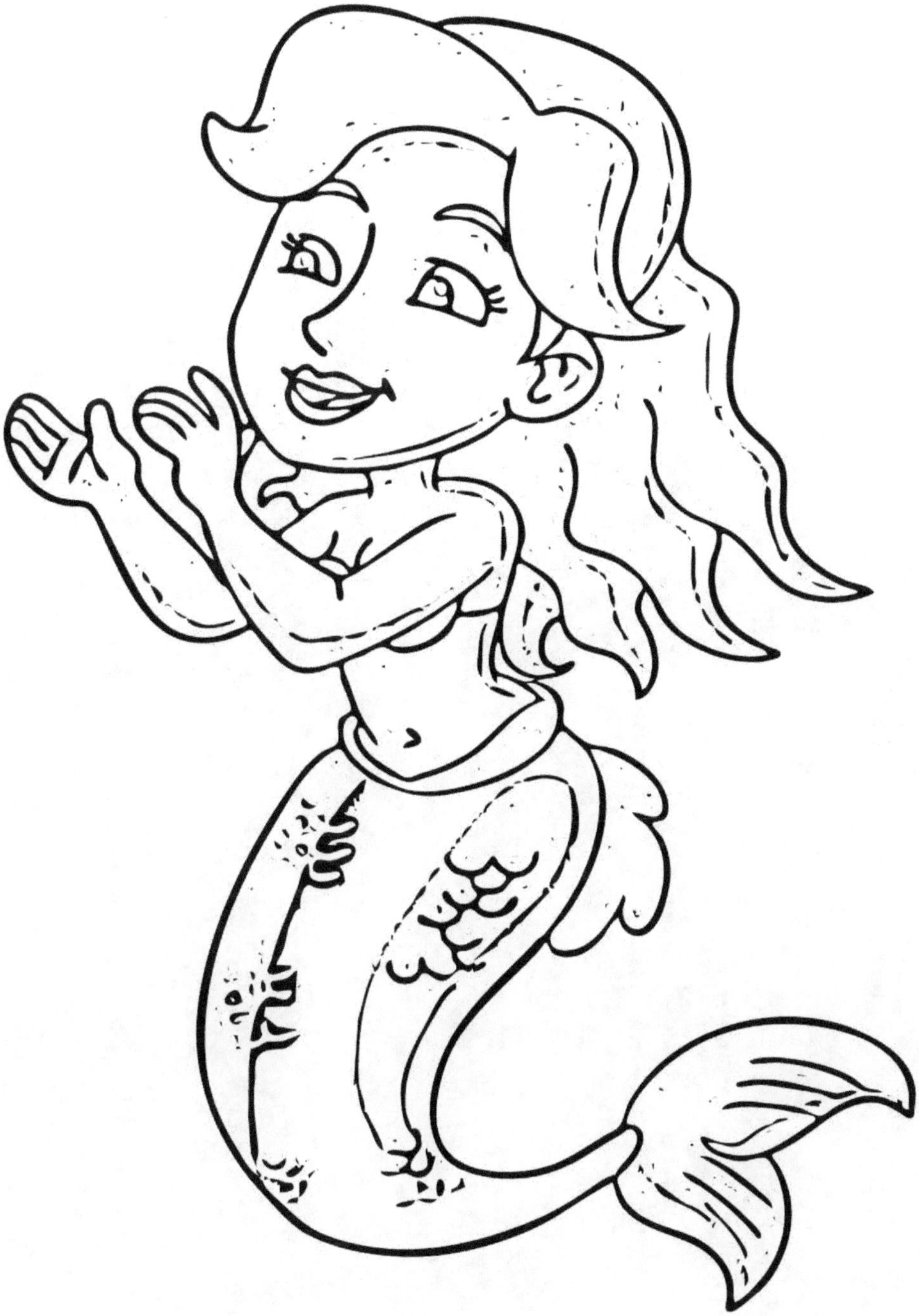

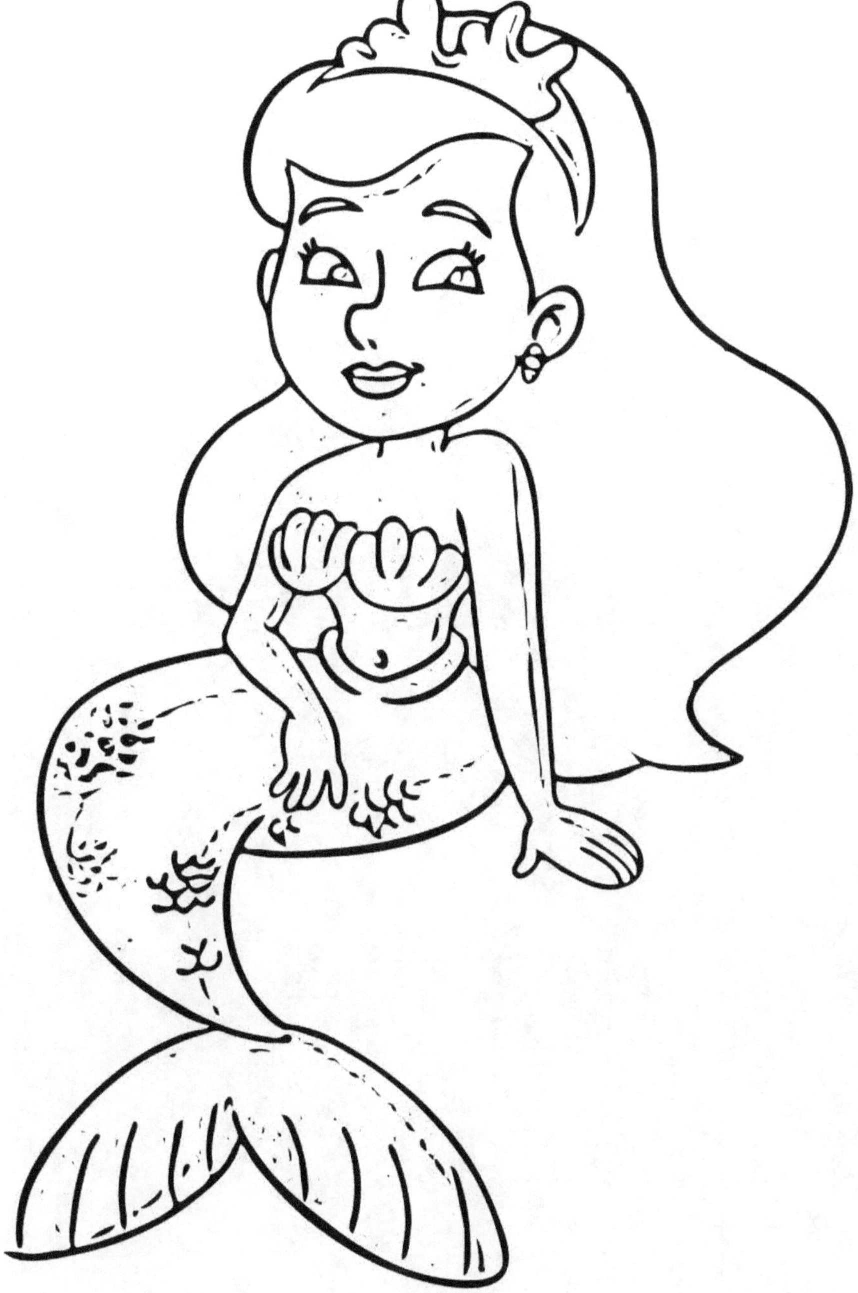

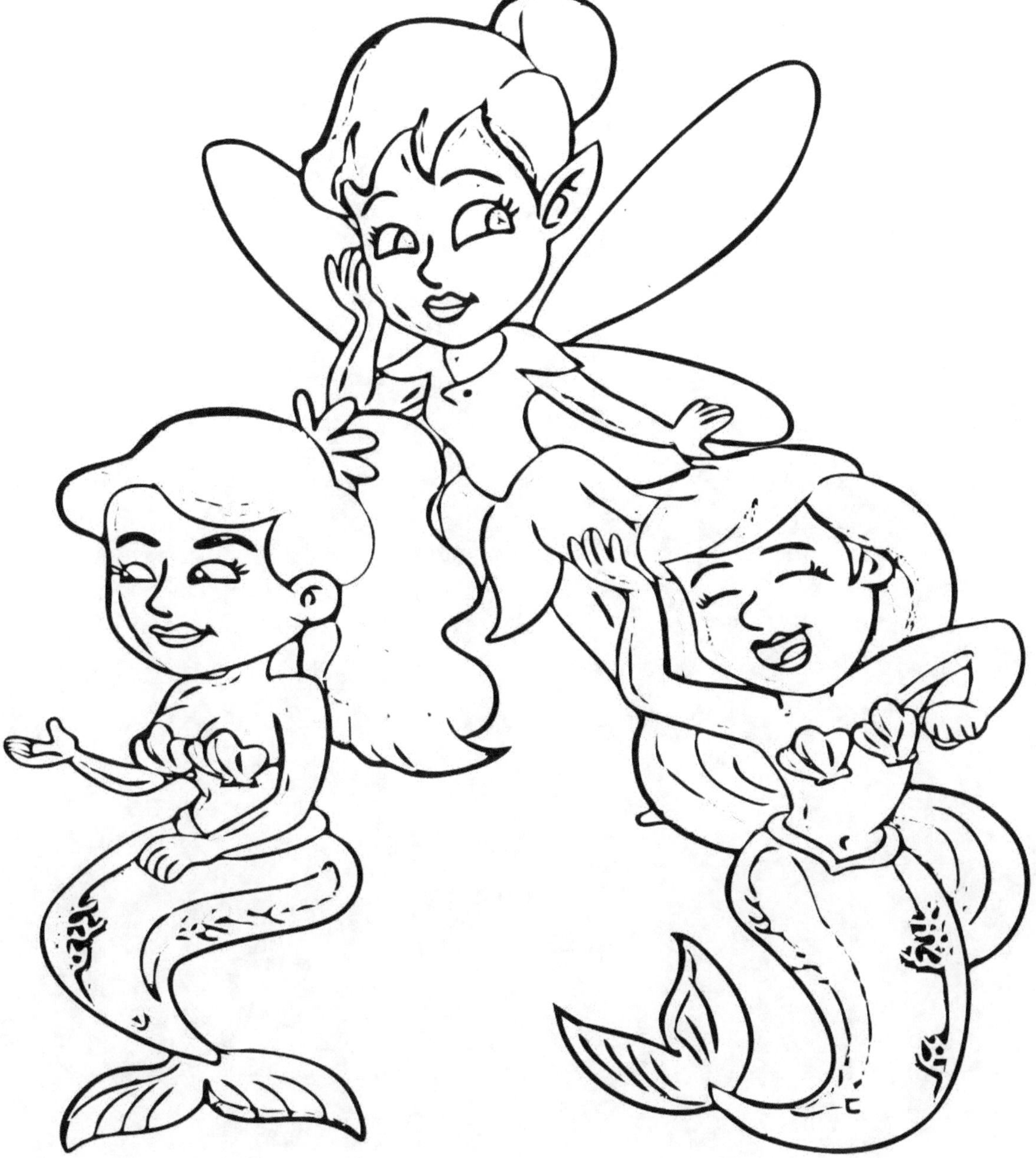

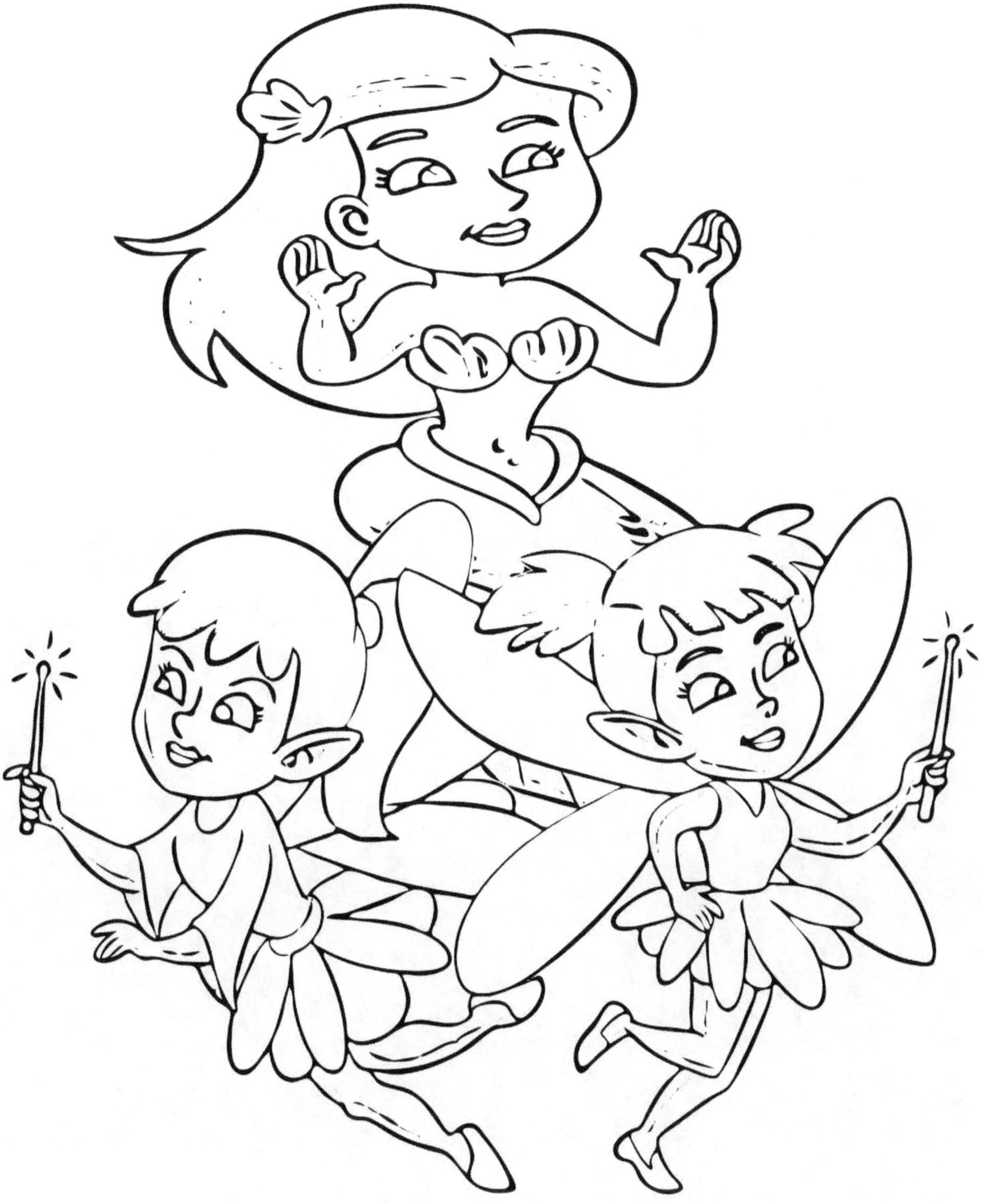

www.ingramcontent.com/pod-product-compliance
Lightning Source LLC
Chambersburg PA
CBHW080618180526
45168CB00007B/2959
9781519247599